Dot Mar

Christmas Activity Book

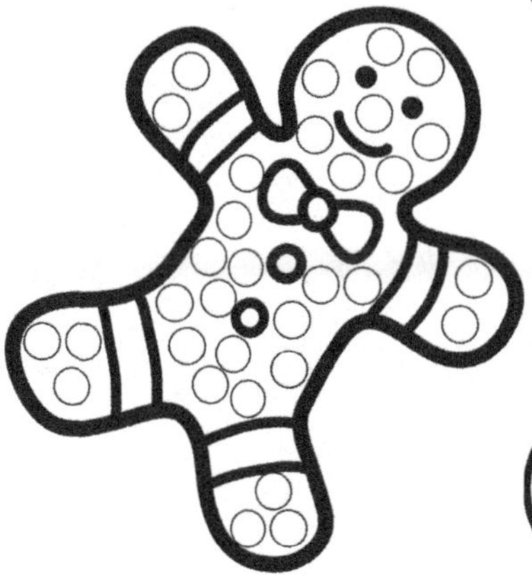

This Book Belongs To:

ho
ho
ho

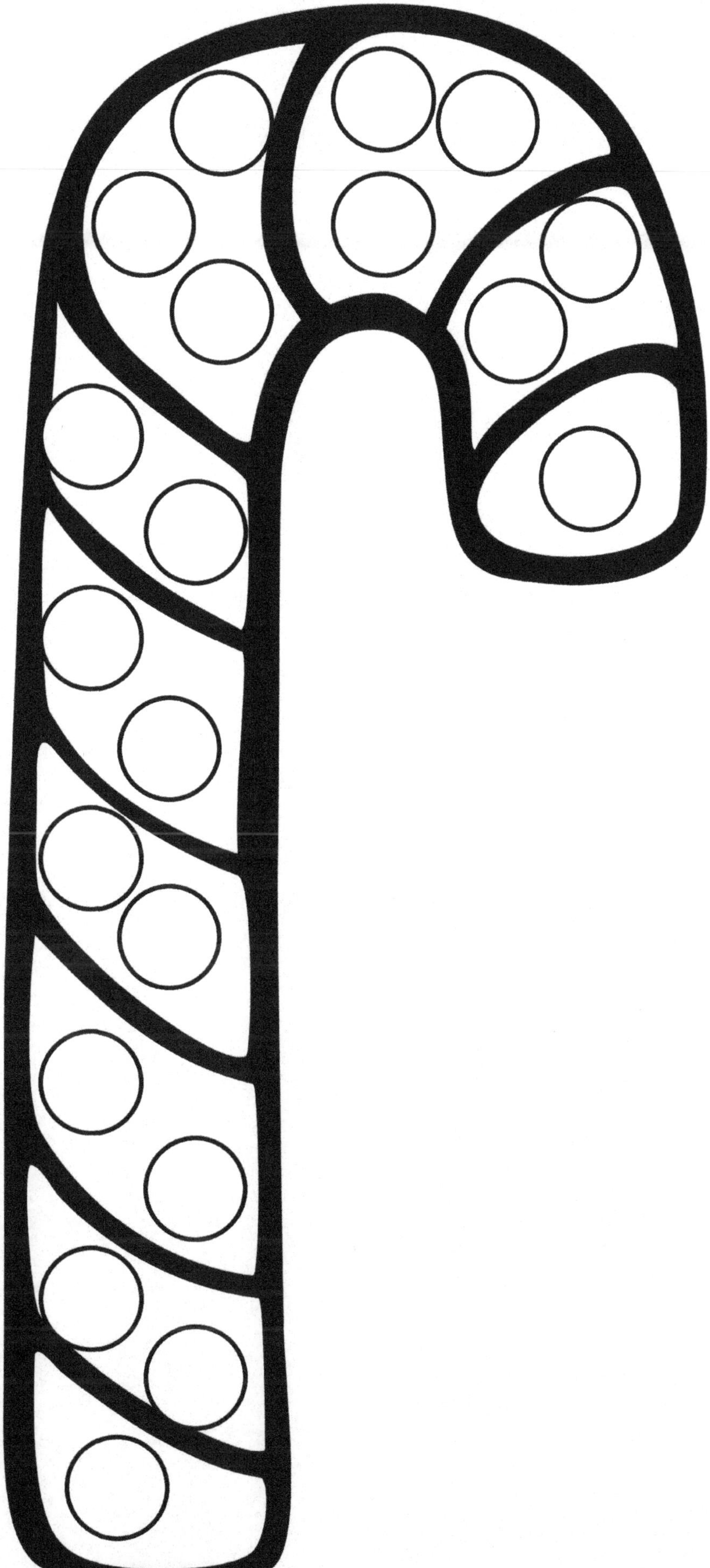

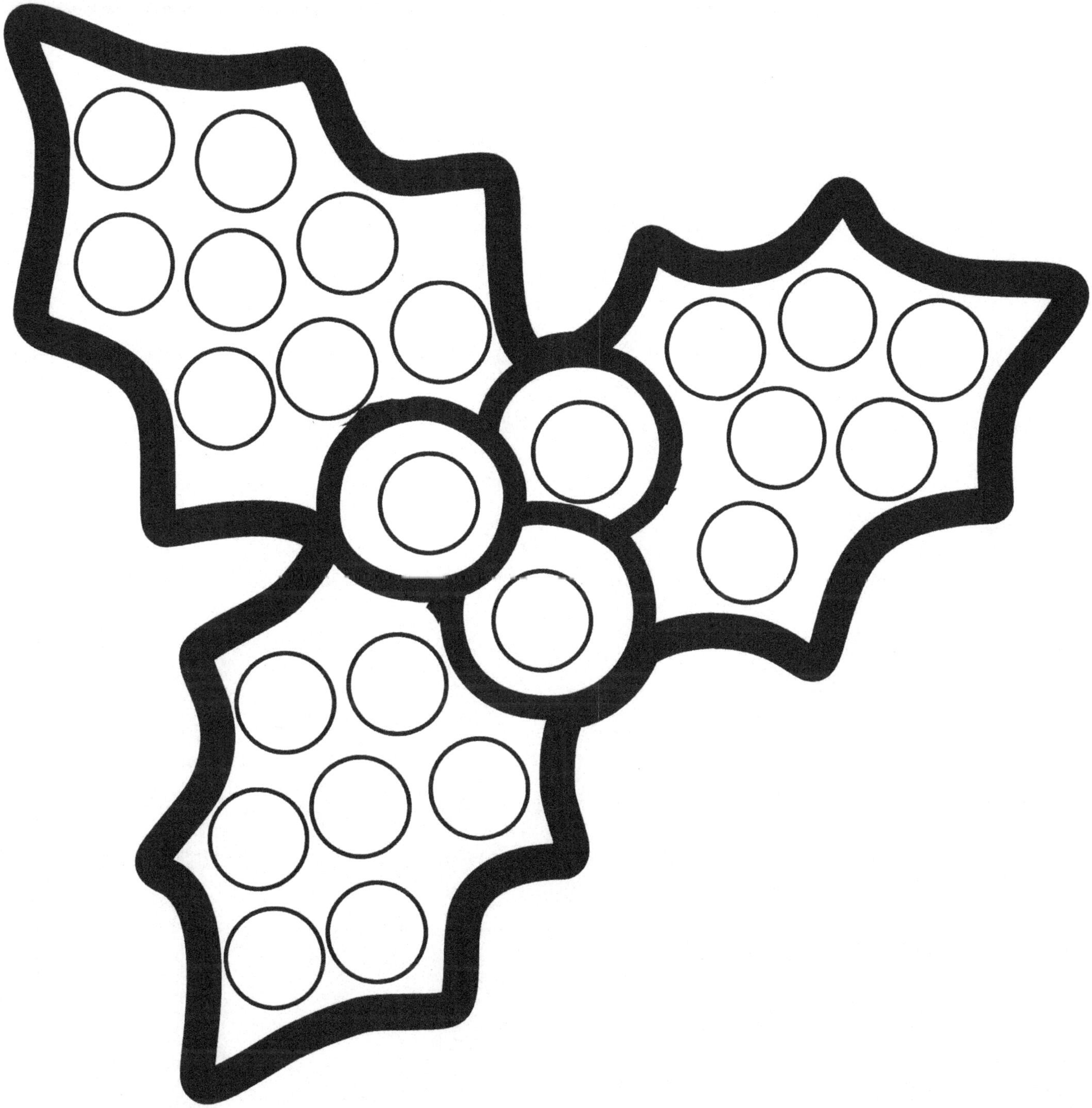

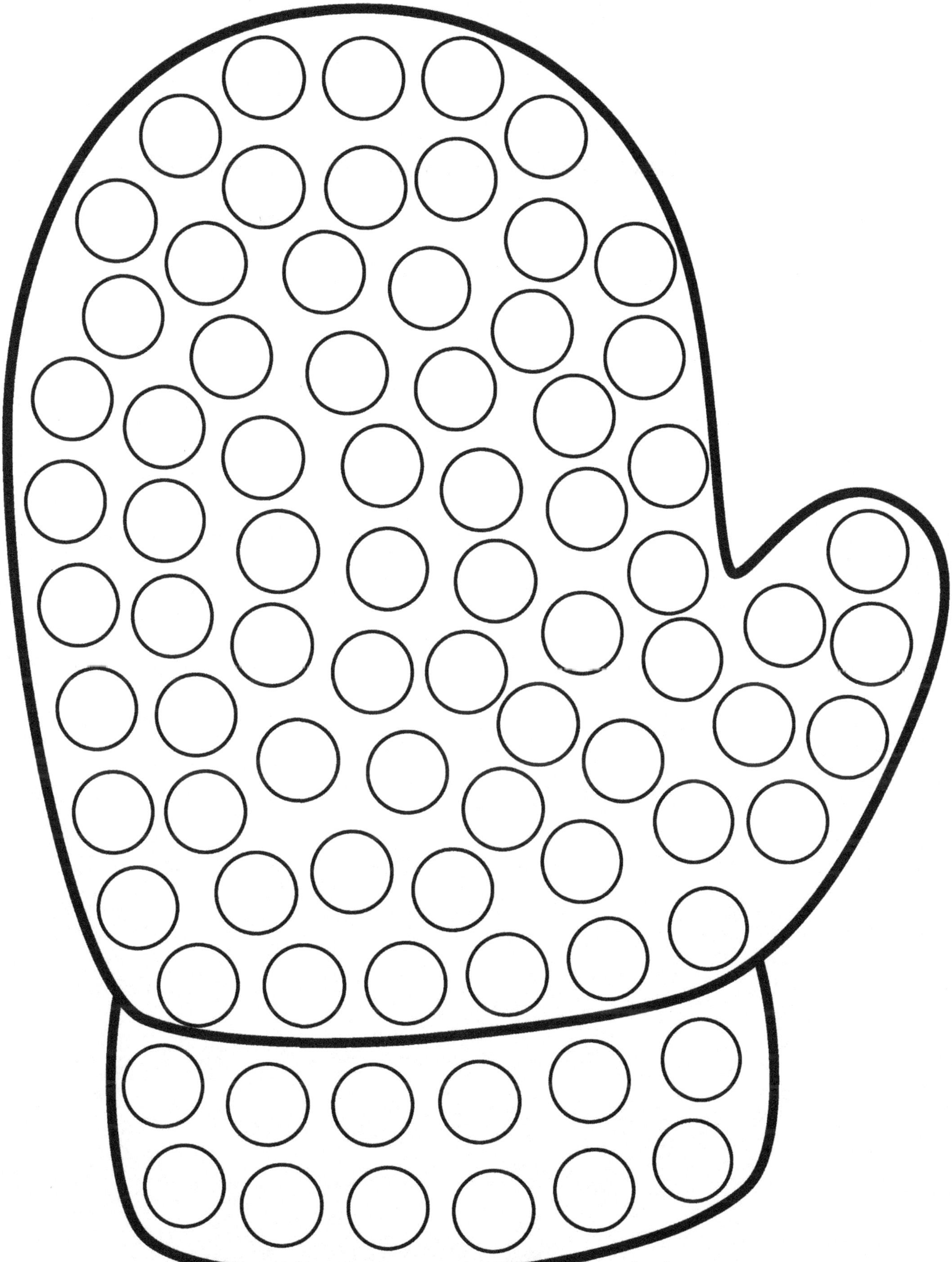

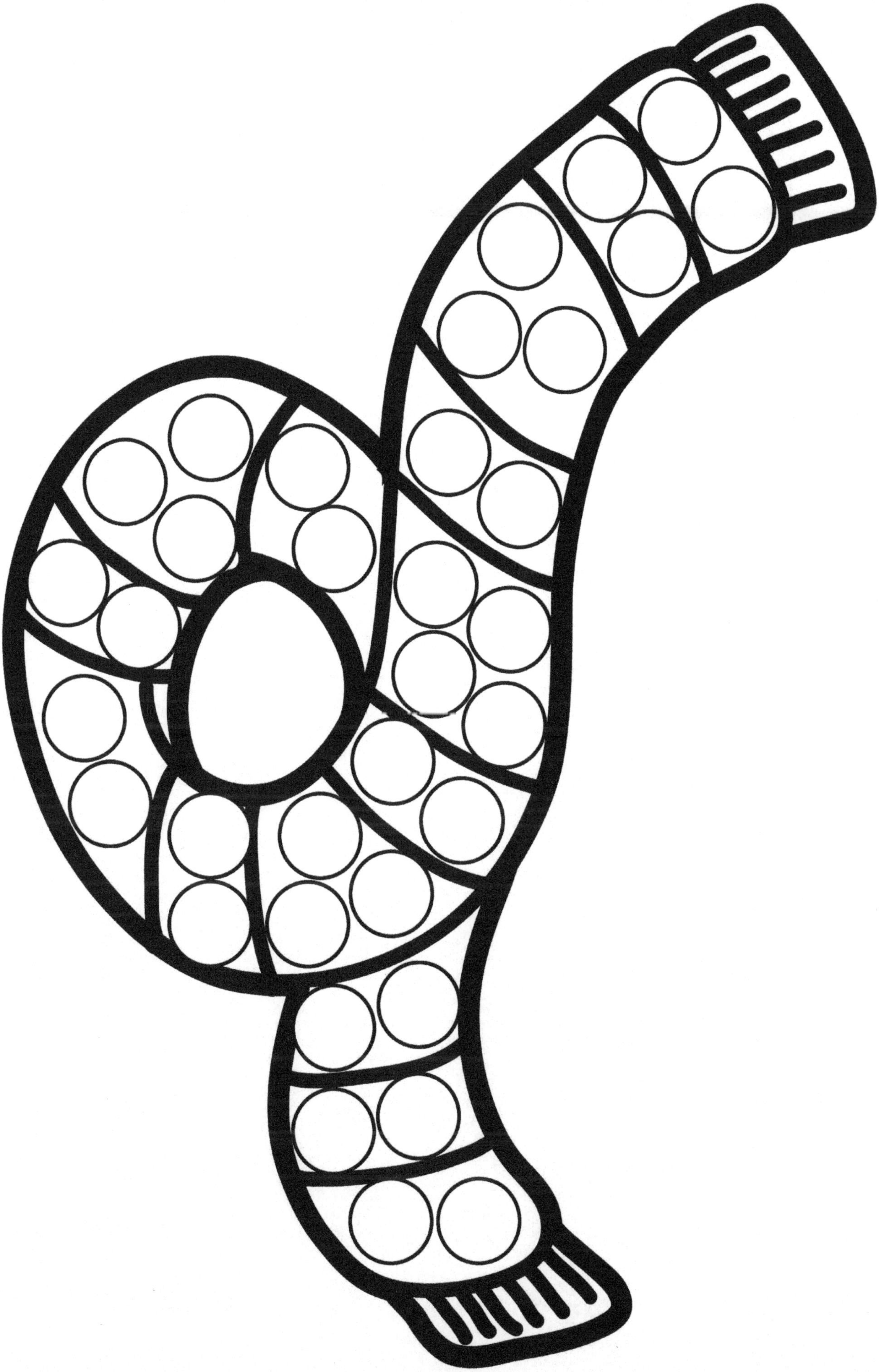

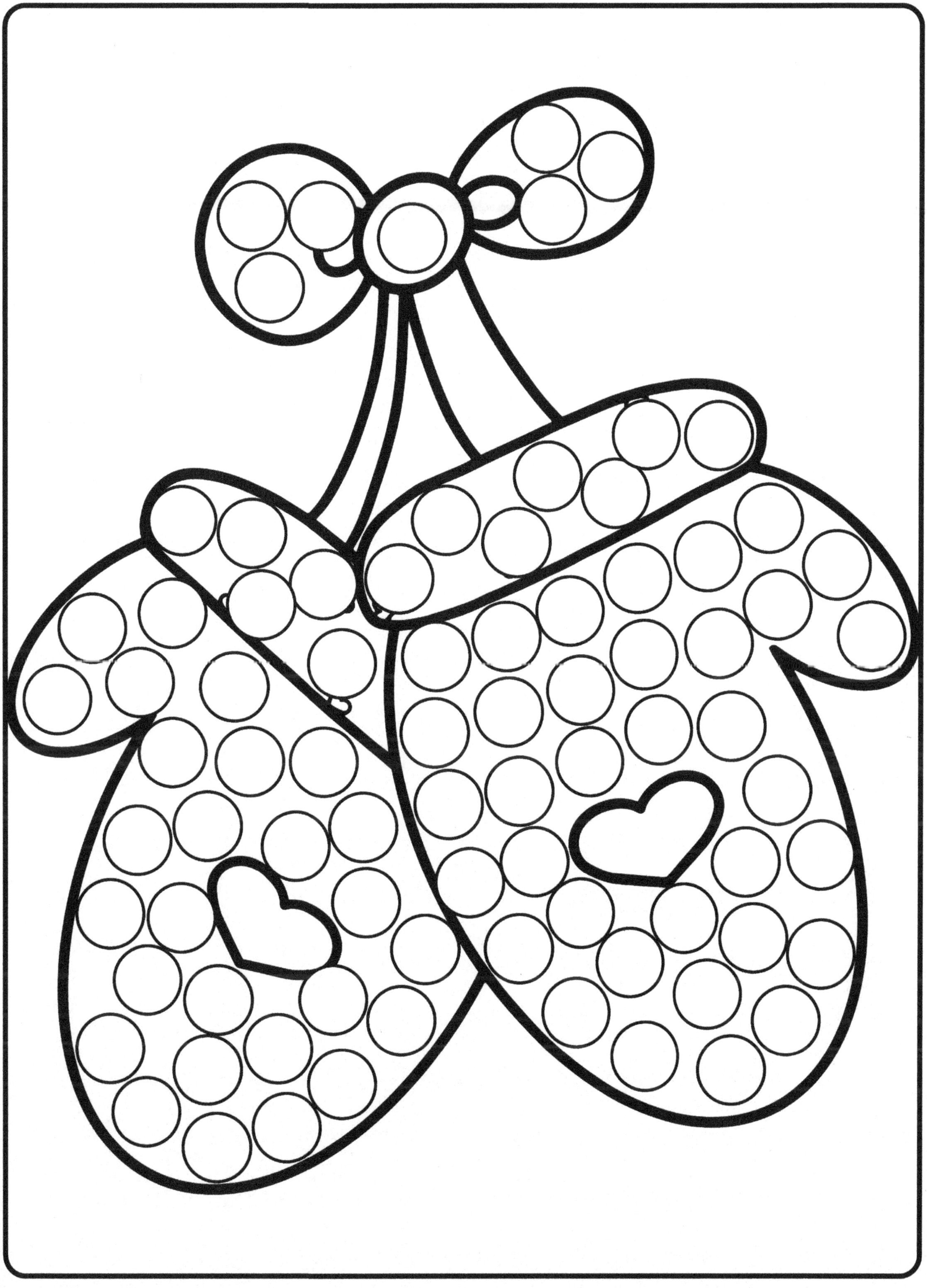

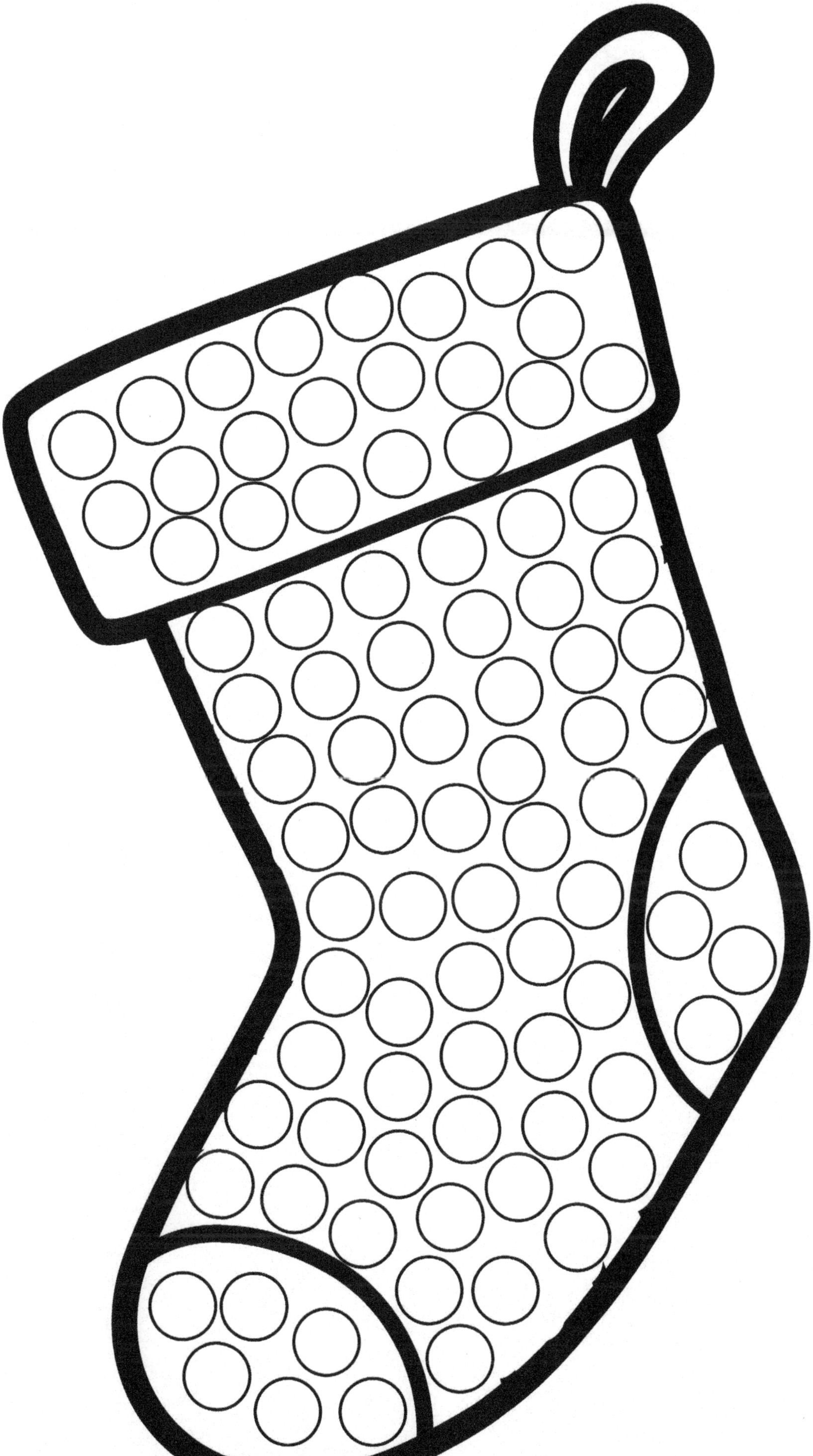